FIRST 50
FINGERSTYLE PATTERNS
YOU SHOULD PLAY ON GUITAR

by Chris Woods

PLAYBACK+
Speed • Pitch • Balance • Loop

To access audio, visit:
www.halleonard.com/mylibrary

Enter Code
7173-8663-0685-1671

ISBN 978-1-5400-9509-1

HAL•LEONARD®

Visit Hal Leonard Online at
www.halleonard.com

World headquarters, contact:
Hal Leonard
7777 West Bluemound Road
Milwaukee, WI 53213
Email: info@halleonard.com

In Europe, contact:
Hal Leonard Europe Limited
1 Red Place
London, W1K 6PL
Email: info@halleonardeurope.com

In Australia, contact:
Hal Leonard Australia Pty. Ltd.
4 Lentara Court
Cheltenham, Victoria, 3192 Australia
Email: info@halleonard.com.au

CONTENTS

PATTERN 1

PERFORMANCE TIP: As with nearly all the examples in the book, the notes in each chord should be allowed to ring out as long as possible. Experiment with how loudly you play each note. Can you make the root notes louder?

HOW TO PLAY IT: The standard way to fingerpick this is with a *p-i-m-a* pattern, which is explained below. Carefully considered *p-i-m-a* fingerings are provided throughout this book, but feel free to make adjustments as needed, or try your own unique approaches.

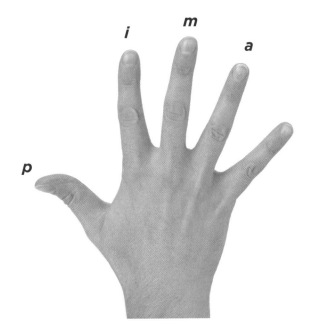

Begin by fretting the entire chord. Then pluck the first note of each bar down with your thumb (*p*). Pluck the second note up with your index finger (*i*), the third note up with your middle finger (*m*), and the final note up with your ring finger (*a*).

In this pattern, the three fingers (*i*, *m*, and *a*) pluck strings 3, 2, and 1, respectively and exclusively. The thumb (*p*) plucks strings 6–4. As is often the case, *p* always plays the root note.

 To access the accompanying audio tracks, simply visit *www.halleonard.com/mylibrary* and enter the code found on page 1 of this book. You can stream or download the tracks at your convenience!

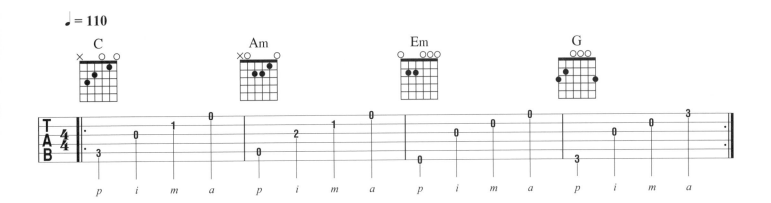

PATTERN 2

A repeated arpeggio pattern mixing eighth and quarter notes, this is perfect for a singer-songwriter, including the likes of Eva Cassidy.

PERFORMANCE TIP: Try counting "1, 2 and, 3, 4." This will help you differentiate between the quarter and eighth notes.

HOW TO PLAY IT: Hold a G chord and pluck string 6 with *p*. This is a quarter note and lasts for the count of "1." The following two notes are eighth notes, which are counted "2 and." Pluck these with *p* on string 4 and *i* on string 3. The last two notes of each bar are quarter notes, counted "3, 4." Pluck these two notes with *m* and *a*, respectively.

Note that, although this pattern is the same for each bar, the bass note changes from string 6 (bar 1) to string 5 (bars 2–4).

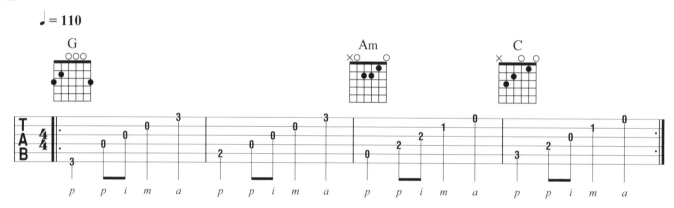

PATTERN 3

This is a "Travis picking" pattern. Travis picking is a technique innovated by guitarist Merle Travis in which the thumb and finger(s) alternate in eighth-note pairs.

PERFORMANCE TIP: Count "1 and, 2 and, 3 and, 4 and." Your thumb (*p*) will pluck on the 1, 2, 3, and 4, and your fingers will pluck on the "ands" in between.

HOW TO PLAY IT: Holding a G chord, alternate *p* and *i* throughout, using *p* for strings 6 and 4 and *i* for string 3. For the C chord, your thumb will move between strings 5 and 4 instead of 6 and 4.

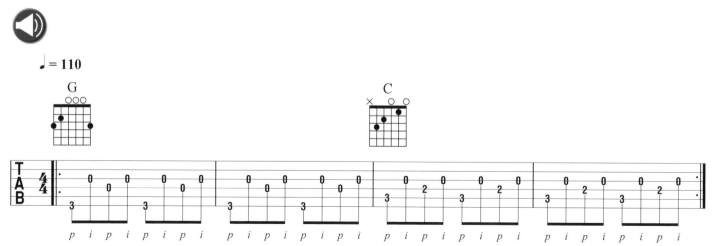

PATTERN 4

Here's an emotive chord sequence with a slightly trickier Travis picking pattern.

PERFORMANCE TIP: Notice how *p* continues to alternate between the root notes (on either string 5 or string 6) and string 4, while the *i* and *m* fingers remain on strings 3 and 2, respectively.

HOW TO PLAY IT: The root notes, again, are really important here. Notice again how the roots will change strings according to each chord.

The first note of each bar is a quarter note played with *p*, which is followed by three eighth-note pairs. This is the essence of the Travis picking technique: alternating between thumb (*p*) and finger (*i* or *m* in this case) in pairs. The first pair is *p* and *i*, the second is *p* and *m*, and the final is again *p* and *i*.

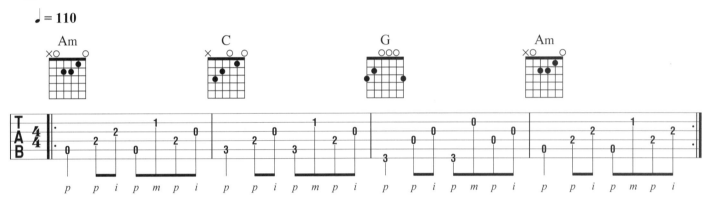

PATTERN 5

An intimate sounding pattern, this is reminiscent of fingerpicking tracks from the likes of Iron and Wine or the Civil Wars.

PERFORMANCE TIP: It's often easier to learn a picking pattern by mastering it on one chord first.

HOW TO PLAY IT: This pattern uses similar chords and ideas to Pattern 3, however, here we're alternating bass notes over three strings, and the pattern lasts two bars.

Begin by playing the root note with *p* on string 6 and follow with *i* on string 3. This pattern of eighth-note pairs continues, with *i* remaining on string 3 throughout while *p* alternates between strings 4 and 5 for the remainder of the two-bar pattern.

At bar 3, the pattern starts over again with *p* playing string 6 on beat 1 before continuing to alternate on strings 4 and 5 again.

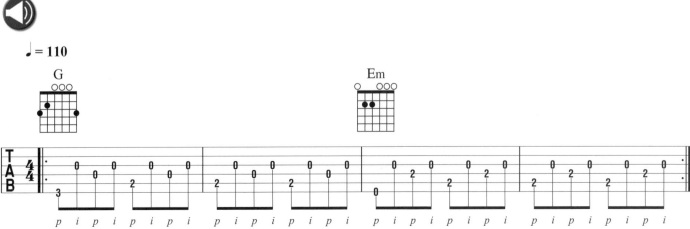

PATTERN 6

A suspended chord pattern popular with Tom Petty and others, this pattern features plucking two strings simultaneously.

PERFORMANCE TIP: When reading fingerpicking patterns, remember to pay attention to the chord symbols above the tab.

HOW TO PLAY IT: Starting with a D major chord, pluck strings 4 and 1 at the same time with *p* and *a*, respectively. The next quarter note needs *p* and *m* on strings 4 and 2, again respectively and simultaneously.

The second half of each bar starts with a pair of eighth notes—pluck string 4 with *p* followed by string 3 with *i*. The final quarter note is simply string 4 plucked with *p*. This pattern then repeats, and we simply change chords to create some harmonic movement.

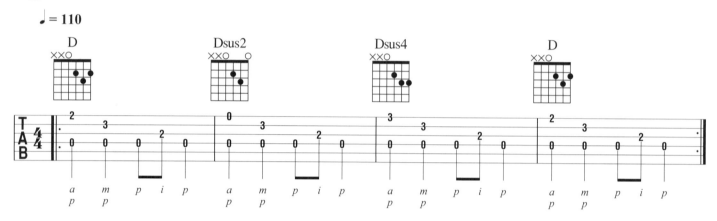

PATTERN 7

Inspired by Americana and country folk artists such as John Prine, this is a variation on the standard Travis picking pattern.

PERFORMANCE TIP: Allow each chord to ring out for the entire bar to create a full sound.

HOW TO PLAY IT: Starting with a familiar C chord, pluck string 5 with *p* and string 2 with *m* at the same time. We'll repeat this simultaneous plucking move—sometimes called a *pinch*—on beat 1 of each bar. The rest of the bar reverts to a standard Travis picking pattern, bouncing between thumb and finger for each pair of eighth notes. Note that each bar finishes with a sole quarter note played with *p*.

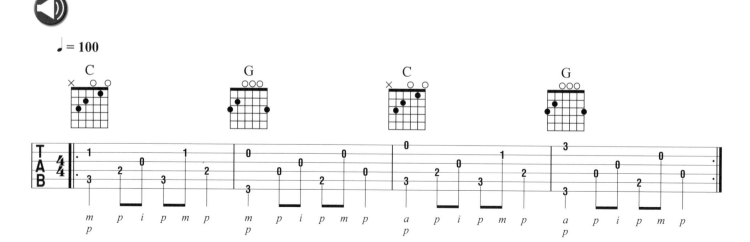

PATTERN 8

This is a slow and slightly sad Travis picking pattern, played in quarter notes instead of eighth notes, that makes use of the *i*, *m*, and *a* fingers.

PERFORMANCE TIP: Notice how the bass line alternates between strings 5 and 4 like many Travis patterns, but the treble line moves in a repeated pattern of string 3 (*i*)–2 (*m*)–1 (*a*)–2 (*m*).

HOW TO PLAY IT: As is often the case, we begin playing the root of the chord with *p*. We follow that with *i* on string 3, *p* on string 4, and finally *m* on string 2. The second bar begins the same with *p* on string 5, but then we follow with *a* on string 1. The second half of the bar is the same as bar 1.

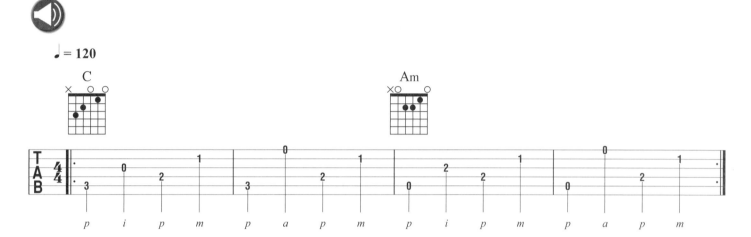

PATTERN 9

A syncopated pattern with a Red Hot Chili Peppers sound, this is a fairly simple sequence with a rhythmic twist.

PERFORMANCE TIP: The sixteenth notes (fourth and fifth notes of the bar) are a new addition. Count "1 and, 2 and *a*" for the first part of the bar.

HOW TO PLAY IT: On beat 1, pluck the open sixth and second strings of the E chord with *p* and *m*, respectively, followed by string 4 with *p*. Beat 2 begins with *i* on string 3 for an eighth note, which is followed by two sixteenths: *p* on string 5 and *a* on string 1. We allow string 1 to ring out until string 2 is plucked on beat 4 with *m*. The syncopation in this pattern is created by allowing the sixteenth note at the end of beat 2 to ring through beat 3.

The same timing is used in bar 2, but the pattern is altered to fit the C chord.

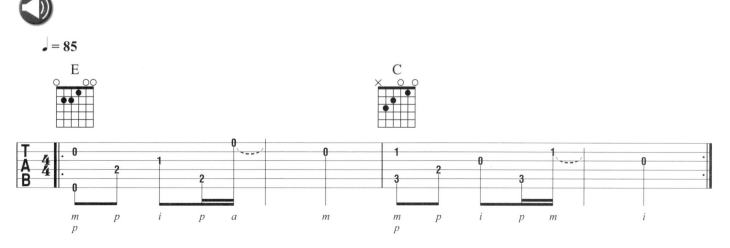

PATTERN 10

This chord sequence is found in countless contemporary hits by bands like Counting Crows and Green Day.

PERFORMANCE TIP: Get used to playing sixteenth notes by starting slowly and counting correctly. In this case, practice counting "1 and a, 2 e and a" to get the pattern right.

HOW TO PLAY IT: Each bar uses the same pattern with the exception of the root note, which moves from string 6 for G5 to string 5 for Cadd9. Begin by plucking the root note with *p* and a melody note on string 2 with *m*. Then follow a Travis pattern across the sixteenth-note pairs, alternating as usual between thumb and finger.

Notice how the pattern restarts halfway through the bar. Everything is exactly the same except the melody note, which has moved from string 2 to 1.

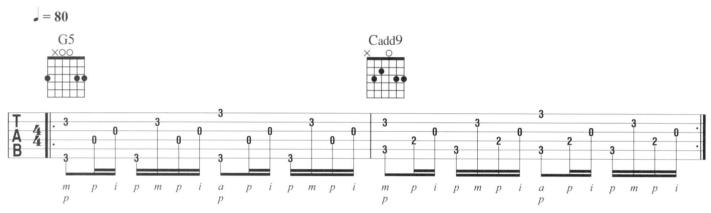

PATTERN 11

A bluesy sevenths sequence, this pattern mixes Travis picking with some plucked dyads.

PERFORMANCE TIP: Pay close attention to how eighth notes cover the beginning and end of the bar. The count is "1 and, 2 e and a, 3 e and a, 4 and."

HOW TO PLAY IT: Using *p*, *m*, and *a*, pluck strings 5, 2, and 1 at the same time, focusing on even volume. Next, pluck strings 3 and 2 with *i* and *m*, respectively. Beats 2 and 3 are comprised of sixteenths and played in the familiar Travis picking style, alternating thumb and finger. The rhythm slows back down to eighth notes again for beat 4.

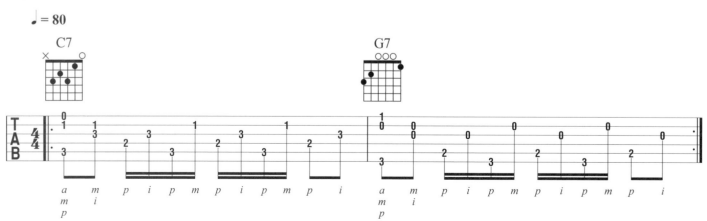

PATTERN 12

This example has a classical guitar feel and sounds a bit like John Williams and Xuefei Yang.

PERFORMANCE TIP: It can be a challenge at first to start on your *a* finger, so focus on keeping the volume of all fingers even and build up to tempo.

HOW TO PLAY IT: Holding a D minor chord, play the descending pattern of four sixteenth notes starting on string 1 with your *a* finger. Then begin to ascend for two eighth notes before plucking the complete D minor chord. We then repeat the same pattern for the second bar with A minor, except *p* has now moved to string 5 for the final A minor chord to give the correct root note.

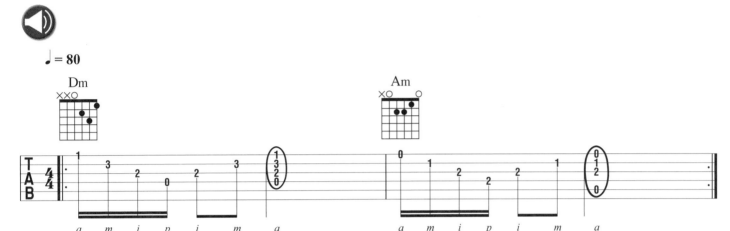

PATTERN 13

A ballad-style pattern, this one is inspired by the rock band the Stereophonics.

PERFORMANCE TIP: Always start super slowly and gradually build up to full tempo at your own pace.

HOW TO PLAY IT: It's important to keep your hammer-ons strong and clear. Play the relevant open string with your picking hand and then snap down a fret-hand finger quickly and forcefully onto the string for the hammer-on. Try to imagine swatting a fly. Line it up, prepare, and then, in a quick and smooth movement, hit down on the target.

This pattern begins with the first finger removed from the chord C so that it can be hammered on. Continue playing the root bass note on the beat with *p* and pluck strings 3 and 2 in between with the fingers. Use your pinky on fret 3 of string 2.

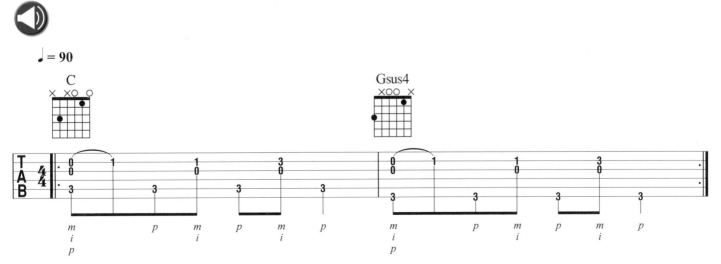

PATTERN 14

Here's a short chordal break inspired by the stylistic playing of John Mayer.

PERFORMANCE TIP: It's not essential to hold down the full barre for the F chord.

HOW TO PLAY IT: Holding an F chord, but with string 3 open, pluck strings 4–2 with *p*, *i*, and *m*, respectively. Hammer your second finger on to string 3 before removing it again and re-plucking the same strings. For the last chord of the bar, shift *p*, *i*, and *m* over to strings 5–3.

In the second bar, this same technique is adapted to the C and G chords. Note that, for the final G chord, you're plucking strings 6, 4, and 3.

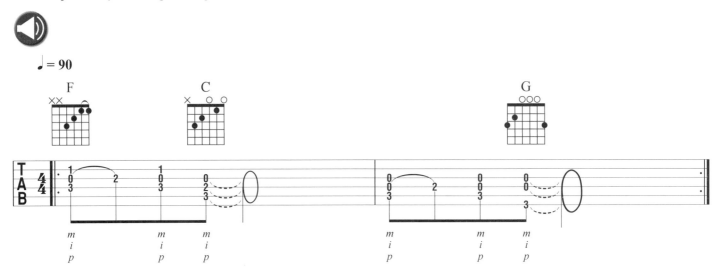

PATTERN 15

A challenging Travis picking pattern with hammer-ons, this is a popular combination with many—from songwriters like Ralph McTell to virtuosos like Chet Atkins.

PERFORMANCE TIP: Plan ahead for the hammer-on, taking a finger away from the chord before you play the relevant note.

HOW TO PLAY IT: Begin by playing the root note of the chord with *p*, followed by strings 4 and 2 simultaneously with *p* and *m*, respectively. Work through the next six notes with a standard Travis pattern. Lift your second finger away from the C chord, pluck the open D string, and then hammer on back to the second fret with that same finger. Maintain the Travis picking order for the remaining three notes, lifting your third finger off the root for the open A bass note, which will lead us to the next bar.

The pattern then adjusts logically for the second bar and G chord, shifting bass notes down one string to work with the root note on string 6. Notice how the treble strings remain the same.

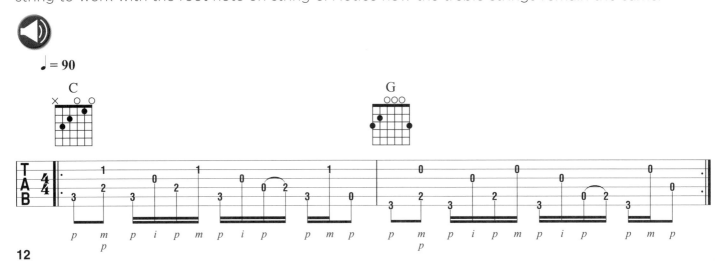

PATTERN 16

Another ballad-themed pattern, this one sounds a bit like Pierre Bensusan and Alex de Grassi, only without the re-tuning.

PERFORMANCE TIP: Pay close attention to how effective it is to let notes ring out across bars.

HOW TO PLAY IT: Holding a standard D chord, pluck strings 4 and 1 and then pull off your second finger to the open first string. Try to let all the notes ring out as long as possible from here on. A simple Travis-picked run of eighth notes leads us through the rest of the bar, which ends with a quarter note on beat 4.

For the second bar, leave the D chord in place and use your second finger for the third fret on string 5. In the final bar, again use your second finger on string 5, adding your pinky for the third fret on string 1.

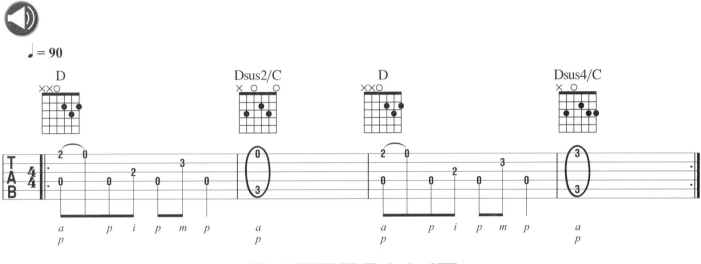

PATTERN 17

With a shuffle feel and a hammer-on pickup note, this is a favorite for players like Davey Graham and Bert Jansch.

PERFORMANCE TIP: Notice this is played with a shuffle (swung eighths) feel.

HOW TO PLAY IT: Begin by plucking the open G string with *i* and hammer on to the second fret as you pluck the open A string with *p*. (You may find it easier to hammer on the entire A minor chord.) After plucking through the chord with *i*, *m*, and *a*, we reach a simplified G chord consisting only of a G note on string 6 (*p*) and the open second string (*m*).

In the second bar, we hold down a thinned-out F chord. After plucking strings 6 and 3 with *p* and *i*, respectively, pluck the open B string with *m* and hammer on to fret 1. Finish with a pinch of open strings 6 and 2 before plucking the open third string, which leads back to the beginning for the repeat.

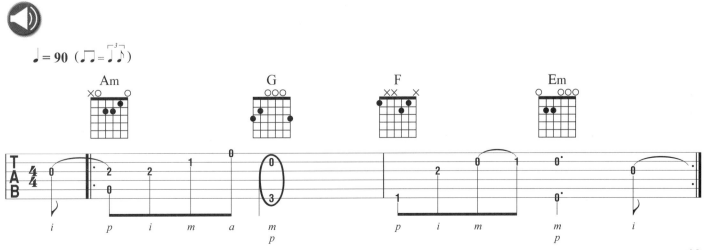

PATTERN 18

Another tricky Travis pattern, this melancholic ballad style features hammer-ons as a repeated motif with an evolving bass.

PERFORMANCE TIP: Technically, we are shifting through three chords, but it can help to simply see this pattern as a C chord with changing bass notes.

HOW TO PLAY IT: As with Pattern 13, you'll need to plan ahead for the hammer-ons, beginning each bar with your first finger lifted off the first fret. The hammer-ons turn this pattern into a steady stream of sixteenth notes. Each bar is the same for the picking hand; only the chord changes.

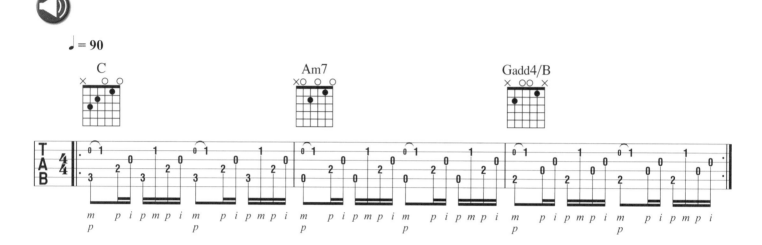

PATTERN 19

Incorporating a percussive string slap with the thumb, this one is reminiscent of Eric Clapton's acoustic work.

PERFORMANCE TIP: If playing a string slap is new to you, take some time to experiment with the motion, making sure to keep it relaxed and natural.

HOW TO PLAY IT: We're using the exact same pattern for every bar here: a repeated sequence of six eighth notes with string slaps on beats 2 and 4. To perform the slap, turn your wrist as if turning a key and slap the side of your thumb against string 6 to create a "click." This mimics a snare drum sound on the backbeat, which is great for creating a one-man groove.

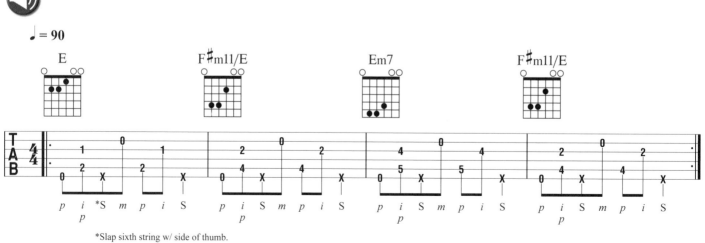

*Slap sixth string w/ side of thumb.

PATTERN 20

This example pairs a country-sounding string slap pattern with a common chord sequence.

PERFORMANCE TIP: Focus on how each string slap is followed by the open G string—almost like a down and up strum motion.

HOW TO PLAY IT: Holding a G chord, begin with a quarter-note root note plucked with *p*. The rest of the bar is straight eighth notes. On beat 2, slap string 6 with the side of your thumb, and then—almost with an upstroke motion—pluck the open G string with *i*. Next, pluck string 5 with *p* and hammer on to the second fret. To close out the bar, beat 4 is the same as beat 2.

Notice how we shift the bass notes up to strings 5 and 4 for the C chord (still using *p*) and simplify the pattern even more in the final bar for the D chord.

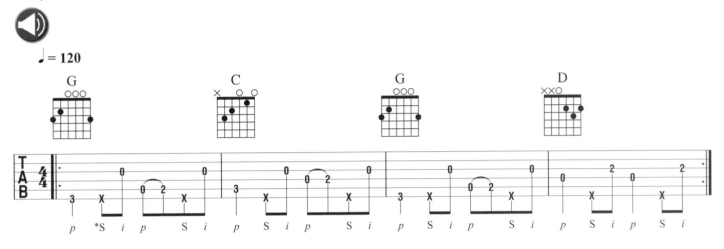

*Slap sixth string w/ side of thumb.

PATTERN 21

In the style of the influential band Extreme, here we're using a simplistic bass, chord, and slap pattern.

PERFORMANCE TIP: With the exception of the last bar, the first six notes are eighth notes, so try counting "1 and, 2 and, 3 and, 4."

HOW TO PLAY IT: To begin, pluck the root note of the chord with *p*, followed by the top three strings with *i*, *m*, and *a* simultaneously. Follow this with the string slap and immediately pluck string 4 with *p*. Beat 3 is sort of a mirror image of beat 1, with the fingers plucking first followed by the thumb. The bar ends with a string slap on beat 4.

The pattern continues in the second bar with the bass notes adjusted to fit the G chord. The final bar uses a popular Dsus4-to-D chord move and concludes with a sustained half-note D chord.

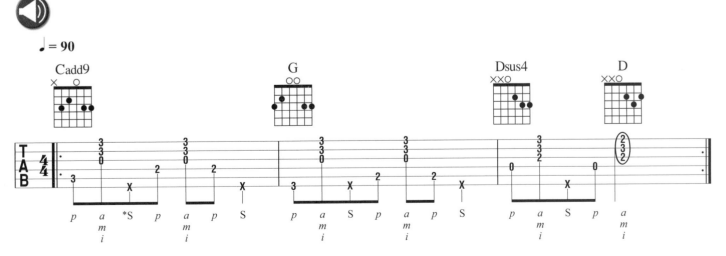

*Slap sixth string w/ side of thumb.

PATTERN 22

A familiar Andy McKee-style groove, this pattern uses a hypnotic chord progression.

PERFORMANCE TIP: Experiment with the "feel," trying to create a sense of groove by playing in a lazy way.

HOW TO PLAY IT: Begin by plucking the first two notes with *p* before plucking strings 3 and 2 with *i* and *m*, respectively. Crucially, this dyad is an eighth note, so it's longer than the previous sixteenth notes. On beat 2, we have a pattern of four sixteenth notes: a string slap (S), a bass note on string 4 (*p*), strings 3 and 2 played together (*i* and *m*), and another bass note on string 4 (*p*).

This two-beat pattern is repeated for the plucking hand throughout as the fret hand changes chords.

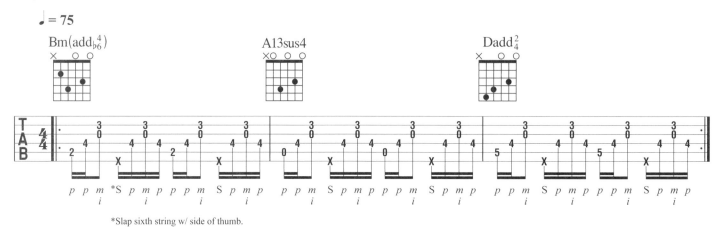

*Slap sixth string w/ side of thumb.

PATTERN 23

This pattern has a relaxed and syncopated feel, emulating the sound of singer-songwriter Tracy Chapman.

PERFORMANCE TIP: Try to focus your slap on string 6 to avoid unintentionally muting other notes.

HOW TO PLAY IT: Begin with a standard D chord but lift your second finger off in preparation for a hammer-on. Pluck all four stings simultaneously, hammer on to fret 2, slap with your thumb on beat 2, and quickly follow by plucking the entire D chord on the "and" of beat 2, which creates a syncopated feel. The chord rings out until beat 4, where we play another string slap.

The pattern is repeated in bar 2—without the hammer-on—and we move through a new voicing of A and a G5 chord.

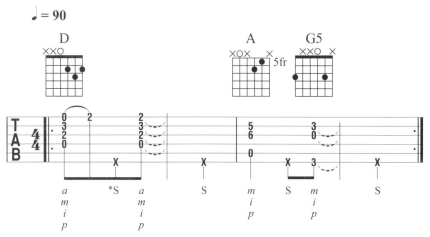

*Slap sixth string w/ side of thumb.

PATTERN 24

A folky and flowing picking pattern consisting of straight eighth notes with a beat-3 string slap, this one is spread across a dreamy chord sequence.

PERFORMANCE TIP: Try to allow the open B string to ring out between chords.

HOW TO PLAY IT: Fret the Emaj7 and pluck the first four notes with *p*, *p*, *i*, and *p*. Then comes our string slap on beat 3, which is followed by strings 5 (*p*), 4 (*p*), and 2 (*m*). Remembering the system of *p* for strings 6–4 and *i*, *m*, and *a* for strings 3, 2, and 1, respectively, will help keep things clear here. The pattern continues across all three bars as the chords change.

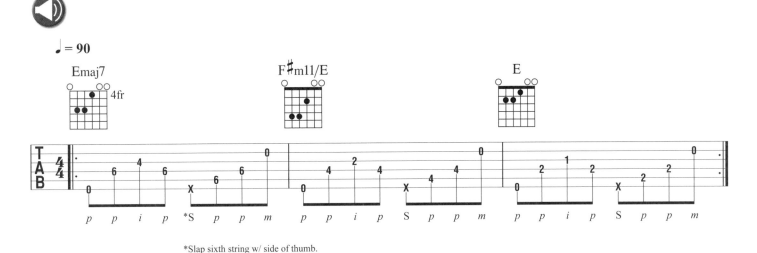

*Slap sixth string w/ side of thumb.

PATTERN 25

The tight syncopation and sweet chords here are reminiscent of an acoustic Ani DiFranco or Dave Matthews track.

PERFORMANCE TIP: The first two chords are where the syncopation lies; control the duration by "squeezing and releasing" the chord.

HOW TO PLAY IT: After plucking the second chord on the "a" of beat 1, release the pressure with your fret hand to mute the chord for the following rest. The rest of the bar is a simple alternation of thumb and finger. The syncopation on beat 1 is best handled by listening rather than counting, but the technique of squeezing and releasing is crucial.

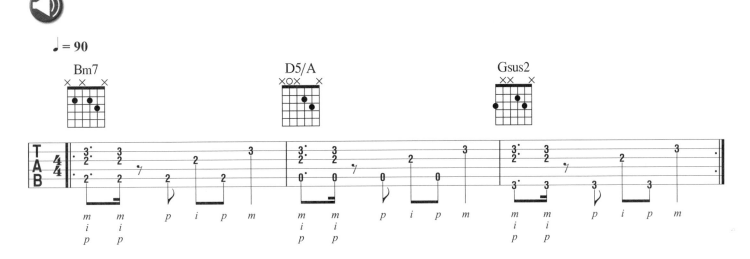

PATTERN 26

A two-bar, slow and swung country blues pattern, this example uses familiar open seventh chords.

PERFORMANCE TIP: Don't forget to "swing" the eighth notes.

HOW TO PLAY IT: The first two notes and the last note of the pattern are quarter notes; sandwiched in between are pairs of eighth notes. We begin with a G7 chord, plucking the root note on string 6 with *p*. Then pluck strings 5 and 2 simultaneously with *p* and *m*, respectively. Finish out the bar with Travis picking on beats 3 and 4. This pattern is interrupted on beat 1 of bar 2 with *a* on string 1 before returning to a Travis picking approach for the remainder of the pattern.

Repeat the pattern for C7 across the last two bars, shifting the bass notes up a string.

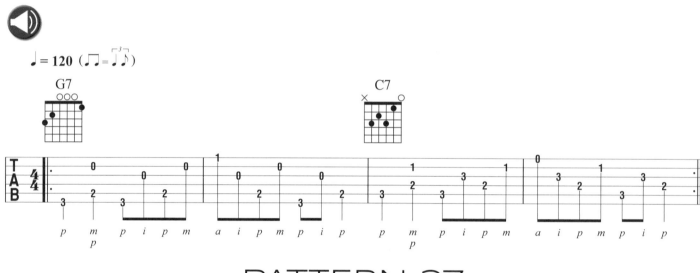

PATTERN 27

A syncopated pattern using chords in a melodic way, this creates a Joni Mitchell-inspired sound without the re-tuning.

PERFORMANCE TIP: Experiment with how you "kill" the bass notes.

HOW TO PLAY IT: Holding down the chord shape, pluck the open A string with *p*. Pluck the following chord tones with *p* and *m*, continuing with *p* on the open A string again. We now come to a crucial rest on beat 3, where you need to "kill" (or mute) the bass note. It sounds great to leave the chord ringing while only stopping the bass note if you can.

To stop the bass note, simply touch it with *p*. Consequently, this prepares you to pluck the final open A string at the end of the bar.

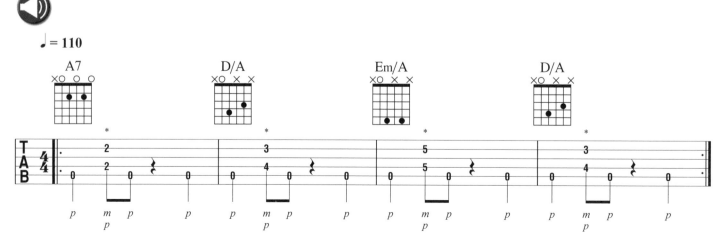

*Allow notes on strings 4 and 2 to sustain through end of measure.

PATTERN 28

In the style of Mason Williams, this pattern combines hammer-ons and pull-offs with an arpeggio riff.

PERFORMANCE TIP: Try to make the volume of your hammer-ons and pull-offs the same as your standard notes.

HOW TO PLAY IT: Form a D chord and pluck strings 4 (*p*) and 1 (*a*) simultaneously. Immediately hammer on to the third fret with your fourth finger and then pull off to the second fret, followed by string 2 plucked with *m*. Finish the bar by plucking string 3 with *i* and string 1 with *a*.

The second bar is a repeated ascending arpeggio riff on strings 5–3 that repeats verbatim in bar 4. Bar 3 is the same as bar 1, save for the last note, which is plucked on string 2.

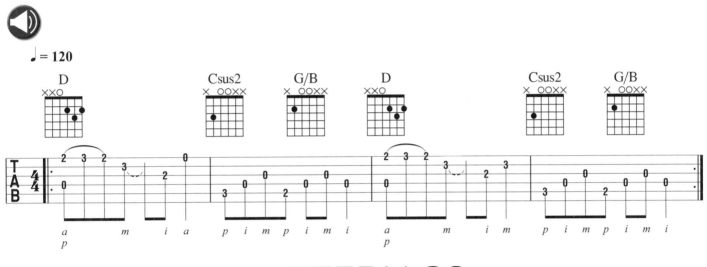

PATTERN 29

A slow swing blues, this pattern is inspired by the rhythm and feel of players such as Lonnie Johnson.

PERFORMANCE TIP: Pay close attention to the rest, as it will help add to the swing feel.

HOW TO PLAY IT: Start things by plucking the root with *p* and then strings 3–1 simultaneously with the remaining fingers. Replant the thumb and fingers on beat 2 to create the rest. Next comes a bass note on string 5 with *p*, the treble strings again—with the addition of our fourth finger on the third fret—plucked with the fingers, and finally a bass note on string 4 with *p*.

This pattern slightly varies on beat 4 in bar 2 and then shifts logically for the A7 chord. Note again the change in voicing of the chord on top for beat 3.

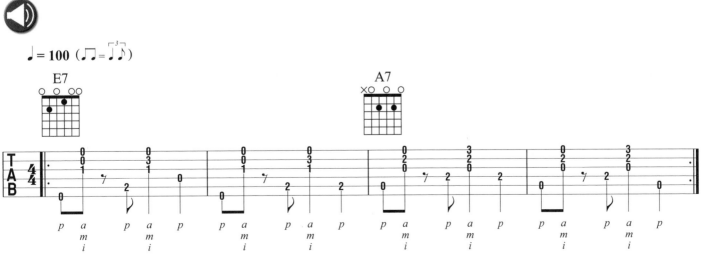

PATTERN 30

This arpeggio pattern has been popular through the years with the likes of '60s folk act Peter, Paul and Mary and other modern acoustic pickers.

PERFORMANCE TIP: The strength of this pattern lies in its bass line; try to emphasize *p* to help with this.

HOW TO PLAY IT: These chords are essentially barre shapes without the barre. Counting "1 2 3, 1 2 3, 1 2," play a pattern of *p-i-m*, *p-i-m*, *p-i*. Your *i* and *m* fingers remain assigned to strings 3 and 2, respectively, while *p* roams the bass strings. Note the slight alteration of the bass-note pattern in bar 2.

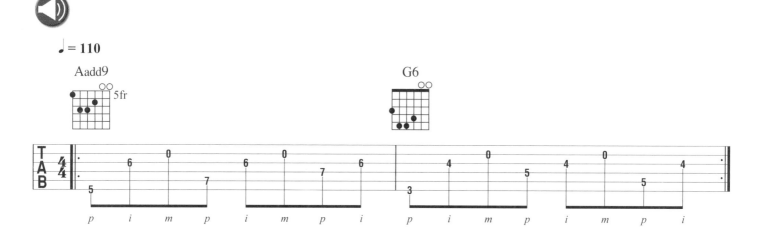

PATTERN 31

Emulating the Celtic-like sounds of Al Petteway, this pattern uses simplified harmonies rather than full chords.

PERFORMANCE TIP: Try to leave the open strings ringing out for as long as possible to create a fuller sound.

HOW TO PLAY IT: Use your second finger for the third-fret G note on string 6, plucking strings 6 and 3 with *p* and *i* simultaneously. Note that *p* rocks back and forth between strings 6 and 4 almost exclusively. The hammer-ons on beat 3 should be fretted with your first finger, and the B minor chord in bar 2 should be fretted with the second and third fingers, low to high. In the final bar, the first fret is best handled with your first finger.

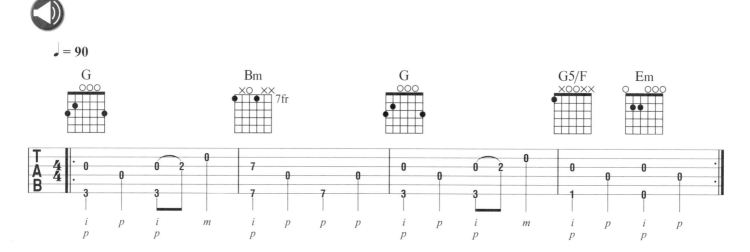

PATTERN 32

A repeated ascending arpeggio, this pattern is reminiscent of Led Zeppelin's acoustic work.

PERFORMANCE TIP: Keep movement to a minimum. Although each bar contains a different chord, many common tones remain throughout.

HOW TO PLAY IT: A fairly easy job for the plucking hand, use a *p-i-m-a* pattern throughout. Regarding the fret hand, use the pinky for all the third-fret notes on string 1. The only tricky spot occurs when moving from bar 1 to bar 2, where you have to swap fingers 3 and 2 for the A minor chords.

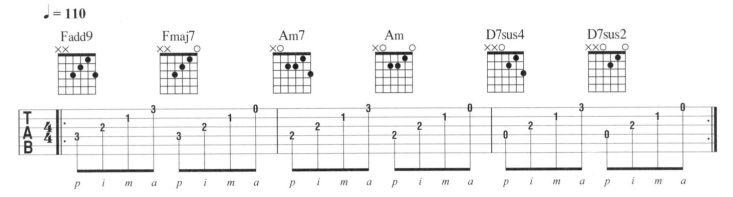

PATTERN 33

This tricky pattern has been utilized by American Primitive player John Fahey.

PERFORMANCE TIP: Listen to the recording to get the feel for the swing rhythm.

HOW TO PLAY IT: For the plucking hand, the first two quarter notes of the bar are repeated, although we do shift root notes with each chord. Beats 3 and 4 can be handled with a Travis approach. The Aadd9 chord can be tricky to finger, so experiment to see what works best.

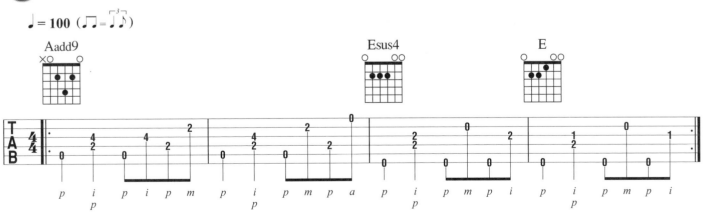

PATTERN 34

A repeated arpeggio with melodic movement within the chord, this pattern is inspired by Radiohead's mellower guitar work.

PERFORMANCE TIP: Try to allow your root note to ring out across the bar.

HOW TO PLAY IT: Fret the bass note on string 6 with your second finger for all three chords and pluck it with *p*. The remaining notes of the arpeggio are handled neatly with *i*, *m*, and *a* for strings 3, 2, and 1, respectively.

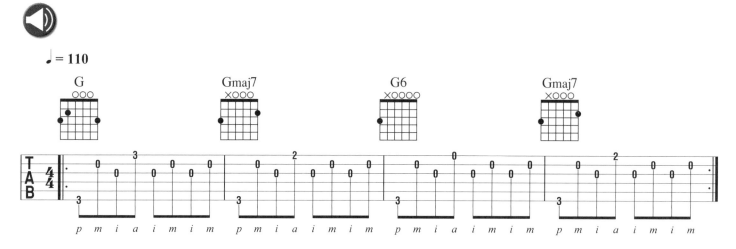

PATTERN 35

A quick, bouncing rhythm with a moving bass, this pattern is influenced by players such as Donovan and Bob Dylan.

PERFORMANCE TIP: Notice how *p* ventures up to string 3, and *i* and *m* are assigned to strings 2 and 1, respectively.

HOW TO PLAY IT: The main pattern lasts for two beats and uses a Travis approach, with *p* bouncing between string 5 and string 3. Most crucially, this is the first time *p* is used on string 3.

The second half of bars 2 and 4 contains a change in the pattern, with two sets of three notes. Each set begins with an eighth note and finishes with two sixteenth notes. Pay attention to how the bass notes move here to connect the two chord roots.

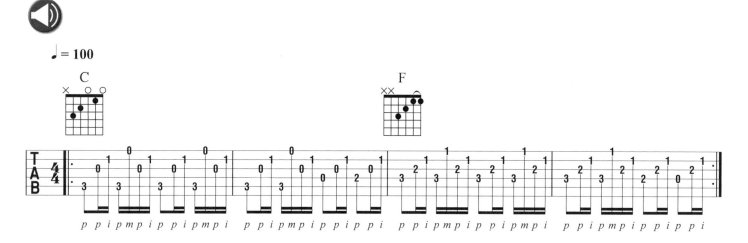

PATTERN 36

PERFORMANCE TIP: Pay close attention to the fingers used to fret and try to plan ahead.

HOW TO PLAY IT: After fretting string 2 with your first finger for the A minor chord and following it with the open D string, fret the G/B chord with fingers 2 and 4, low to high.

The second bar begins with your first finger on the first fret and third finger on the third fret. After the open first string, fret the G5 chord with your third (string 6) and fourth (string 2) fingers. Regarding the plucking hand, use *p* for the bass notes on strings 6–4 and *m* (string 2) and *a* (string 1) for the treble notes.

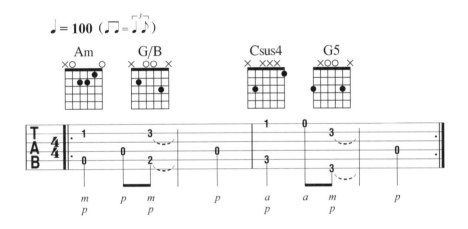

PATTERN 37

PERFORMANCE TIP: The rest is crucial to creating a syncopated feel, so be sure to practice muting the chord.

HOW TO PLAY IT: Be ready to fret an A minor chord directly after plucking the open A and D strings with *p*. Then, use *p* once more to pluck string 4 with the chord fretted. To sound the chord, try "flicking" your finger (or fingers) down (toward the floor) to strum the strings. To stop the chord from ringing into beat 3, release the pressure in your fretting hand and plant your plucking fingers on the strings. This is followed by two melody notes, handled by *m* and *a* (bar 1) or *m* and *i* (bar 2).

*Flick strings in a downward motion w/ R.H. finger(s).

PATTERN 38

Originally a classical guitar approach, this type of arpeggio pattern is now widely used by bands like Metallica.

PERFORMANCE TIP: Plan ahead regarding your fretting fingers for the smoothest sound.

HOW TO PLAY IT: This is a very logically laid out pattern. Your thumb will only be plucking string 6 throughout, and the *i*, *m*, and *a* fingers will remain assigned to strings 3, 2, and 1, respectively. Regarding the fretting hand, if you begin each bar using your third finger, you'll be in good position for the hammer-ons.

♩ = 100

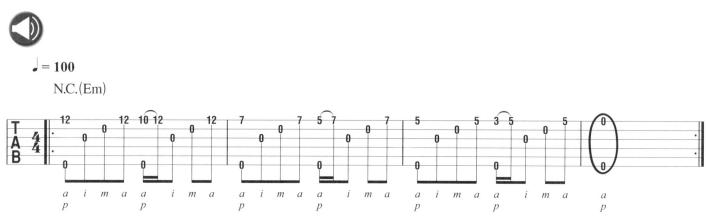

PATTERN 39

Using the 6/8 time signature to create a hypnotic arpeggio, this pattern is inspired by ballads from bands such as REM.

PERFORMANCE TIP: Count "**1** 2 3, **4** 5 6," with an emphasis on 1 and 4 to get the feel of 6/8.

HOW TO PLAY IT: For the first three bars, we're using a simple rolling pattern of *p-i-m-a-m-i*, with the thumb and each finger assigned to one string. The final bar breaks the pattern, using *p-i-m* twice in a row, with the thumb moving to string 5 the second time.

Notice that your fretting-hand first finger can remain on fret 1, string 2 the entire time.

♩ = 110

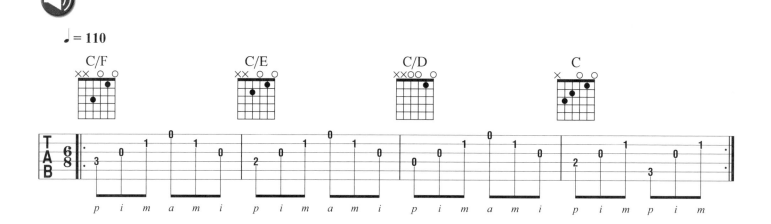

PATTERN 40

This is a magical-sounding sequence with a quarter-note triplet break in the style of contemporary fingerstyle pickers like Don Ross.

PERFORMANCE TIP: The Dadd2/4 chord can be simply thought of as a C chord moved up two frets.

HOW TO PLAY IT: Fretting your Dadd2/4 chord, pluck the root note on string 5 with *p*, allowing the thumb to glide down and also pluck string 4. Follow this immediately with *i* and *m* for strings 3 and 2, respectively. Next, slap string 6 (S) with the thumb, and again pluck strings 3 and 2 together with the fingers as before. The bar finishes with a final string slap on beat 4.

In bar 2, we arpeggiate through the chord in quarter-note triplets. To get a feel for this rhythm, try listening to the audio track rather than trying to count. Bars 3 and 4 are the same as 1 and 2, only moved two frets down for the C chord.

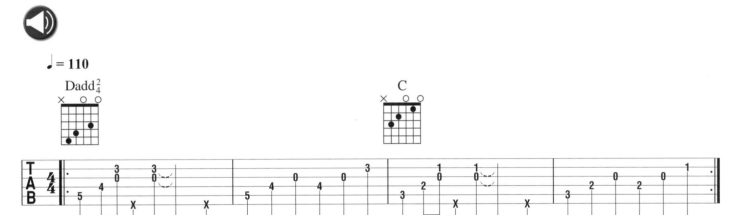

PATTERN 41

Influenced by the finger stylings of John D. Loudermilk, this pattern brings together a strong alternating bass with Travis picking.

PERFORMANCE TIP: Play the first bar until completely confident before moving on.

HOW TO PLAY IT: The first bar sets the theme for this pattern with *p* moving in a pattern of strings 5-4-6-4. This is the bass line and is consistent throughout.

In bar 2, we apply this bass line to Travis picking on an A chord, mixing eighth and quarter notes. Bar 3 is the same as 2 except for the addition of the D note on string 2 (fret 3) to form an Asus4 chord halfway through. Pluck this note with *m* while *p* plucks string 6.

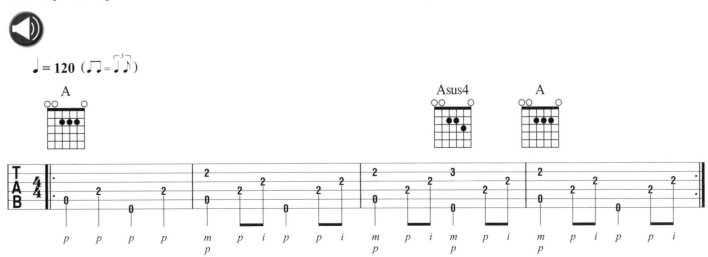

PATTERN 42

This "dead thumb" pattern emulates the blues stylings of Big Bill Broonzy and many more.

PERFORMANCE TIP: Start slowly. No matter how advanced you are, the key to the "dead thumb" technique is working slowly at first until it becomes automatic.

HOW TO PLAY IT: As with the previous pattern, the first bar sets up the bass line for the whole pattern. To create the staccato effect, pluck the open sixth string with *p* and immediately replant *p* so that the string stops vibrating and kills the note. Do this for beats 1–3, allowing beat 4 to ring out normally.

In bars 2 and 3, we then place an open high E string between the first two bass notes followed by a harmony note on beat 2—both plucked with *a*. Bar 2 finishes with the open first string on beat 3 (plucked with *a*), whereas bar 3 finishes with the open second string (plucked with *m*).

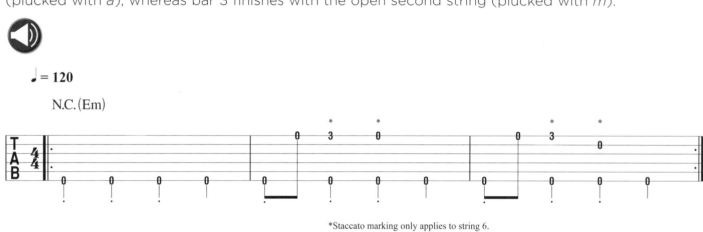

*Staccato marking only applies to string 6.

PATTERN 43

This pattern features a delicate fingerstyle motif inspired by James Taylor.

PERFORMANCE TIP: Halfway through the first bar, briefly fret an E major chord.

HOW TO PLAY IT: After plucking octave A notes on strings 5 (*p*) and 3 (*i*), slide the third-string note up to the fourth fret, back down to the second fret, and then continue to the first fret. Next, form an E major chord, plucking strings 6 and 3 with *p* and *i*, respectively. This is followed with *p* on string 4 and *i* once again on string 3.

Bar 1 ends as it began, with A notes on strings 5 (open) and 3 (second fret). On the second beat of bar 2, re-form your E major chord for the last few notes.

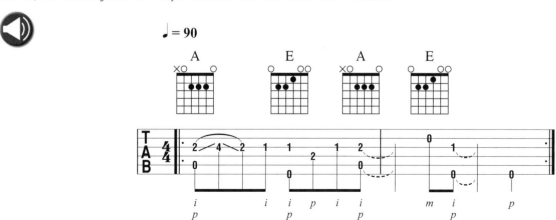

PATTERN 44

Here's a hypnotic pattern using the 3/4 time signature.

PERFORMANCE TIP: If you're not familiar with playing in 3/4, be sure to count "1, 2, 3" throughout the bar to help.

HOW TO PLAY IT: The first two bars set the scene for the pattern. In bar 1, we're simply playing on each beat, beginning with the root note. As usual, *p* is controlling strings 6–4, while *i* and *m* are assigned to strings 3 and 2, respectively.

Bar 2 begins with a string slap on beat 1, continuing with two eighth notes on beat 2 before finishing with strings 3 and 2 played together on beat 3.

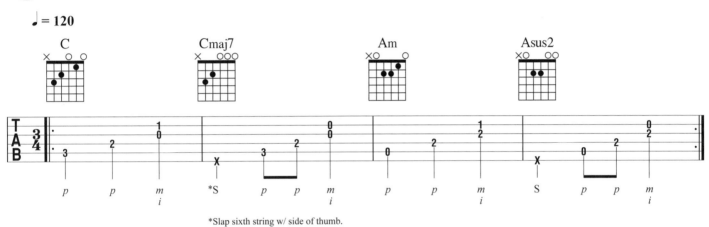

*Slap sixth string w/ side of thumb.

PATTERN 45

A cascading, ascending, and descending arpeggio, this one is reminiscent of Simon and Garfunkel and other '60s folk-infused acts.

PERFORMANCE TIP: Focus on the dynamic control of each note. In other words, be aware of the volume produced with each plucking finger.

HOW TO PLAY IT: Fretting an A major chord, the pattern begins with two eighth notes; the rest of the bar is straight sixteenth notes. Though we begin this stream of notes with a Travis approach, we progress in beat 3 to more cascading arpeggios using only the fingers. Keep the *i*, *m*, and *a* fingers assigned to strings 3, 2, and 1, respectively.

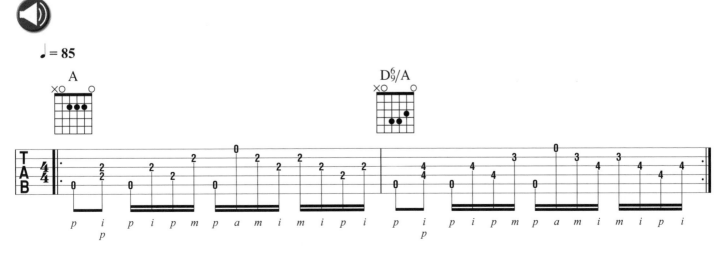

PATTERN 46

Inspired by the techniques of acoustic pioneer Michael Hedges, this example combines a repeated hammer-on/pull-off movement with left- and right-hand independence.

PERFORMANCE TIP: When playing such repetitive movements, keeping the hand relaxed is really important. Remember to start slowly!

HOW TO PLAY IT: Your picking hand will only be plucking a few open strings. This means the sound from any fretted notes will be exclusively generated by your fretting hand and the repeated hammer-on and pull-off movement. Concentrate on the timing so that the plucking and hammer-ons occur simultaneously. It's tricky, so take it super slowly at first.

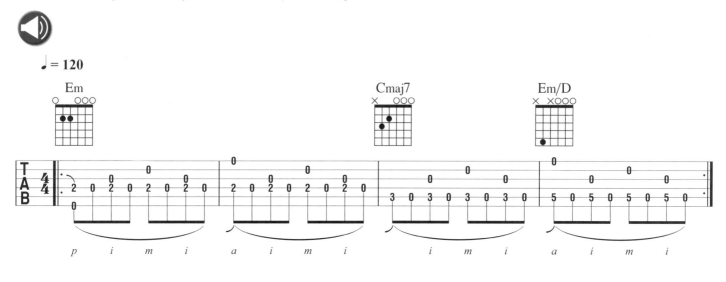

PATTERN 47

This is a cheery Mississippi John Hurt-style pattern utilizing hammer-ons and syncopation to create a bouncing feel.

PERFORMANCE TIP: Try to make the hammer-ons the same volume as the plucked notes to create an even sound.

HOW TO PLAY IT: The first bar is made up exclusively of sixteenth notes, so it can help to count "1 e and a," etc. It's important that your hammer-ons are timed evenly so all the notes—whether plucked or hammered—are the same duration. Standard Travis picking applies here.

Bar 2 is far more rhythmically complex with a mix of sixteenth and eighth notes. We also begin with a hammer-on to B (fret 2), which deviates from our C chord. Practice each bar independently first. In bar 2, try counting "1 e and, 2 and, 3 e and, 4 and."

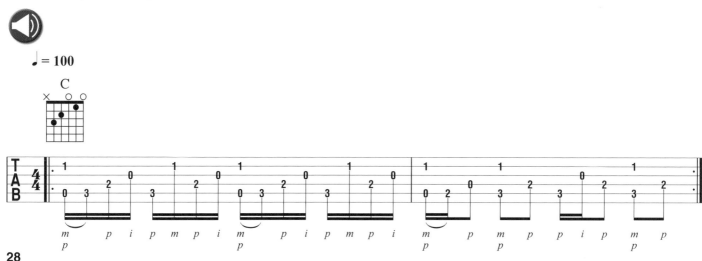

PATTERN 48

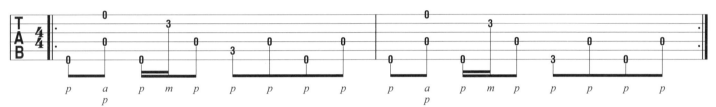

A driving Leo Kottke-inspired pattern, this one is in drop D tuning.

PERFORMANCE TIP: If this is your first time tuning to drop D, try simply playing your open D string and slowly slackening your low E until it sounds the same as your D string.

HOW TO PLAY IT: Begin by playing the open sixth string, followed by strings 4 and 1 simultaneously—all open. Beat 2 is the trickiest, as we have a sixteenth note on string 2 (plucked by *m*) in between two *p* bass notes. Try to let the notes ring out in between to create a Leo Kottke-style sound.

Drop D tuning:
(low to high) D-A-D-G-B-E

♩ = 100

N.C.(D)

PATTERN 49

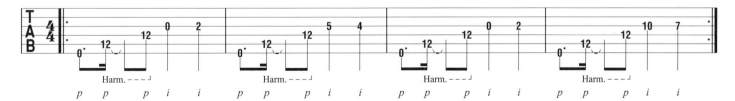

Another one in drop D tuning, the harmonics here create a sound reminiscent of folk innovator Nick Drake.

PERFORMANCE TIP: When playing the harmonics, rest your fretting finger lightly on the string directly over the fret wire for the best sound.

HOW TO PLAY IT: Each bar begins the same, with the open sixth string followed by twelfth-fret harmonics on strings 5 and 4. Use *p* for all of these notes. This is followed with two standard notes (varied each bar) plucked with *i* on string 3. Try to let strings 6–4 ring out and pay attention to the audio to get the rhythm right.

Drop D tuning:
(low to high) D-A-D-G-B-E

♩ = 100

N.C.(Dm)

PATTERN 50

PERFORMANCE TIP: Try emphasizing *p* to punctuate the triplet pattern.

HOW TO PLAY IT: Pay attention to how your picking hand has to shift position as we use the same *p-m-i* pattern on two different string sets. Let the strings ring out as much as possible to create a full and vibrant sound.

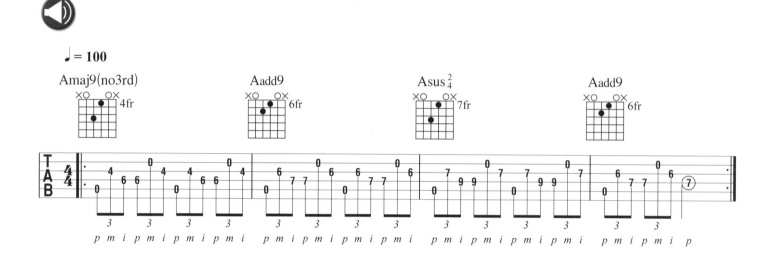

ABOUT THE AUTHOR

Chris Woods is a UK-based guitarist, composer, and educator. Recording as "The Chris Woods Groove Orchestra," he is renowned as an explorer of the guitar, always pushing the boundaries of the instrument. A fingerstyle virtuoso with a love for inspiring others.

www.chriswoodsgroove.co.uk

RHYTHM TAB LEGEND

Rhythm Tab is a form of notation that adds rhythmic values to the traditional tab staff.

TABLATURE graphically represents the guitar fingerboard. Each horizontal line represents a string, and each number represents a fret. Rhythmic values are shown using ovals, stems, and dots.

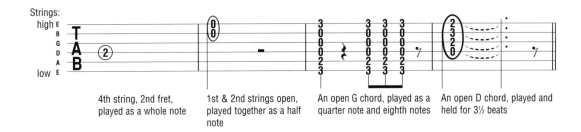

| 4th string, 2nd fret, played as a whole note | 1st & 2nd strings open, played together as a half note | An open G chord, played as a quarter note and eighth notes | An open D chord, played and held for 3½ beats |

Definitions for Special Guitar Notation

HALF-STEP BEND: Strike the note and bend up 1/2 step.

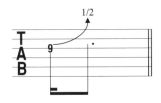

WHOLE-STEP BEND: Strike the note and bend up one step.

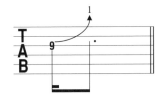

SLIGHT (MICROTONE) BEND: Strike the note and bend up 1/4 step.

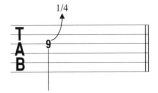

BEND AND RELEASE: Strike the note and bend up as indicated, then release back to the original note. Only the first note is struck.

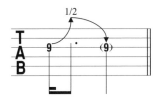

PRE-BEND: Bend the note as indicated, then strike it.

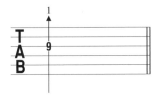

GRACE NOTE PRE-BEND AND RELEASE: Bend the note as indicated. Strike it and release the bend back to the original note.

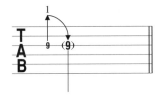

UNISON BEND: Strike the two notes simultaneously and bend the lower note up to the pitch of the higher.

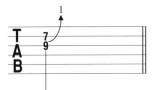

HOLD BEND: While sustaining bent note, strike note on different string.

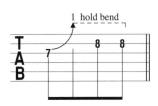

VIBRATO: The string is vibrated by rapidly bending and releasing the note with the fretting hand.

WIDE VIBRATO: The pitch is varied to a greater degree by vibrating with the fretting hand.

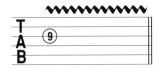

HAMMER-ON: Strike the first (lower) note with one finger, then sound the higher note (on the same string) with another finger by fretting it without picking.

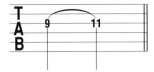

PULL-OFF: Place both fingers on the notes to be sounded. Strike the first note and without picking, pull the finger off to sound the second (lower) note.

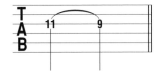

HAMMER FROM NOWHERE: Sound note(s) by hammering with fret hand finger only.

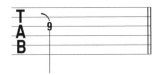

GRACE NOTE SLUR: Strike the note and immediately hammer-on (or pull-off) as indicated.

GRACE NOTE SLUR (CLUSTER): Strike the notes and immediately hammer-on (or pull-off) as indicated.

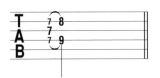

LEGATO SLIDE: Strike the first note and then slide the same fret-hand finger up or down to the second note. The second note is not struck.

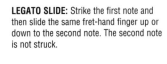
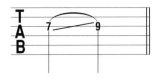

SHIFT SLIDE: Same as legato slide, except the second note is struck.

GRACE NOTE SLIDE: Quickly slide into the note from below or above.

TRILL: Very rapidly alternate between the notes indicated by continuously hammering on and pulling off.

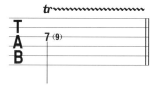

TAPPING: Hammer ("tap") the fret indicated with the pick-hand index or middle finger and pull off to the note fretted by the fret hand.

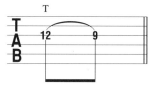

NATURAL HARMONIC: Strike the note while the fret-hand lightly touches the string directly over the fret indicated.

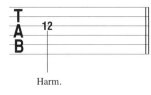

PINCH HARMONIC: The note is fretted normally and a harmonic is produced by adding the edge of the thumb or the tip of the index finger of the pick hand to the normal pick attack.

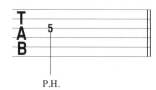

HARP HARMONIC: The note is fretted normally and a harmonic is produced by gently resting the pick hand's index finger directly above the indicated fret (in parentheses) while the pick hand's thumb or pick assists by plucking the appropriate string.

PICK SCRAPE: The edge of the pick is rubbed down (or up) the string, producing a scratchy sound.

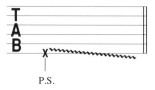

MUFFLED STRINGS: A percussive sound is produced by laying the fret hand across the string(s) without depressing, and striking them with the pick hand.

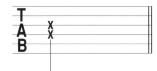

PALM MUTING: The note is partially muted by the pick hand lightly touching the string(s) just before the bridge.

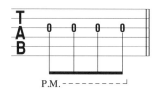

RAKE: Drag the pick across the strings indicated with a single motion.

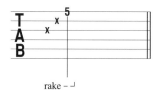

TREMOLO PICKING: The note is picked as rapidly and continuously as possible.

ARPEGGIATE: Play the notes of the chord indicated by quickly rolling them from bottom to top.

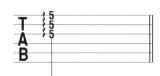

VIBRATO BAR DIVE AND RETURN: The pitch of the note or chord is dropped a specified number of steps (in rhythm), then returned to the original pitch.

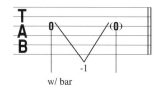

VIBRATO BAR SCOOP: Depress the bar just before striking the note, then quickly release the bar.

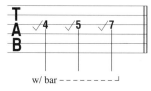

VIBRATO BAR DIP: Strike the note and then immediately drop a specified number of steps, then release back to the original pitch.

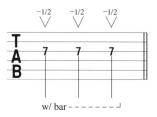

Additional Musical Definitions

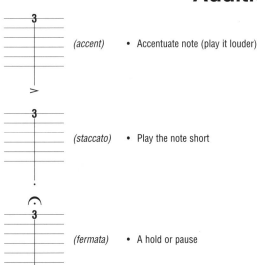

(accent) • Accentuate note (play it louder)

(staccato) • Play the note short

(fermata) • A hold or pause

⊓ • Downstroke

∨ • Upstroke

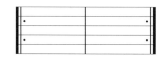

• Repeat measures between signs

NOTE: Tablature numbers in parentheses are used when:
• The note is sustained, but a new articulation begins (such as a hammer-on, pull-off, slide, or bend), or
• A bend is released.
• A note sustains while crossing from one staff to another.